09-BTO-533

UN WEAPONS INSPECTORS

By Cory Gunderson

VISIT US AT
WWW.ABDOPUB.COM

Published by ABDO & Daughters, an imprint of ABDO Publishing Company, 4940 Viking Drive, Suite 622, Edina, Minnesota 55435.

Printed in the United States.

Edited by: Sheila Rivera
Contributing Editors: Paul Joseph, Chris Schafer
Graphic Design: Arturo Leyva
Cover Design: Castaneda Dunham, Inc.
Photos: Corbis, Fotosearch

Library of Congress Cataloging-in-Publication Data

Gunderson, Cory Gideon.
U.N. weapons inspectors / Cory Gunderson.
p. cm. -- (World in conflict--Middle East)
Includes index.
Contents: Overview of U.N. weapons inspectors -- Role of the United Nations -- The inspection process -- The 1990s U.N. weapons inspectors of Iraq -- U.N. weapons inspections in Iraq in the 21st century -- Other U.N. weapons inspections.
ISBN 1-59197-414-3
1. Persian Gulf War, 1991--Juvenile literature. 2. Weapons--Inspection--Iraq--Juvenile literature. 3. United Nations--Iraq--Juvenile literature. [1. Persian Gulf War, 1991. 2. Weapons--Inspection--Iraq. 3. United Nations--Iraq.] I. Title. II. World in conflict (Edina, Minn.). Middle East.

DS79.723.G86 2003
341.5'8--dc21

2003040[illegible]

TABLE OF CONTENTS

Overview of UN Weapons Inspectors 5

Role of the United Nations 12

The Inspection Process 21

The 1990s UN Weapons Inspections of Iraq 23

UN Weapons Inspections in the 21st Century 29

Other UN Weapons Inspections 36

Web Sites 39

Timeline 40

Fast Facts 42

Glossary 44

Index 48

The devastating power of modern day weapons

Overview of UN Weapons Inspectors

The future may see a time when such a [nuclear] weapon may be constructed in secret and used suddenly and effectively with devastating power by a willful nation or group against an unsuspecting nation or group of much greater size and material power.

-U.S. Secretary of War Henry Stimson to Harry Truman in April of 1945

Much has changed since the September 11, 2001, terrorist attacks against the United States. One of these changes is the way the U.S. deals with threats to its safety. Now the U.S. doesn't wait to react to harm caused by enemies. The U.S. government works to prevent as much of that destruction as possible.

U.S. President George W. Bush spoke to the United Nations, or UN, on September 12, 2002. The UN is made up of people from many countries. These UN team members work to

The September 11, 2001, terrorist attack on the World Trade Center in New York

ensure peace and safety for all people. In his speech, Bush urged the UN to be firm with Iraq. He wanted to take action against Saddam Hussein's government in Iraq. President Bush described Hussein's rule as a "grave and gathering danger."

President Bush and several U.S. presidents before him have been concerned about Iraq. They think Saddam's government has the potential to harm other countries. These presidents believed that Saddam built up enough weapons to cause great world destruction. President Bush believes this, too.

The U.S. wanted the support of other countries as it dealt with Iraq. The UN could provide the broad support of many countries. The UN's main purpose is to maintain worldwide peace. Its leaders make sure that weapons of mass destruction are removed, disarmed, and/or destroyed. These weapons have the potential to kill many at one time. The UN hoped to prevent another war between the U.S. and Iraq. Teams of UN weapons inspectors prepared to go into Iraq late in 2002. Their job was to rid Iraq of weapons of mass destruction.

UN weapons inspectors had searched Iraq before. In April of 1991, Iraq accepted a UN resolution, or formal statement. The resolution required the country to end its weapons of mass destruction program. Under pressure, the Iraqi government

A ground-to-air missile launching military tank

accepted this. Iraq allowed the UN to monitor and make sure they no longer had these weapons.

The inspections that began in 1991 and continued until 1998 did not go smoothly. There was friction between the Iraqi government and the UN weapons inspectors.

The 2002-2003 UN weapons inspectors in Iraq likely faced some of the same difficulties as those who inspected before them. The jobs of both inspection teams were the same. They had to rid Iraq of weapons of mass destruction. The inspectors were also to prevent potential violence, including the possibility of war.

A portrait of Iraqi President Saddam Hussein

ROLE OF THE UNITED NATIONS

Before the UN was formed, the League of Nations existed. The League of Nations began in 1919 to promote cooperation between nations. Their goal was to achieve peace and security. When this organization failed to prevent the Second World War, it stopped its work. The organization ceased to exist.

Former U.S. President Franklin D. Roosevelt came up with the name "United Nations" in 1942. During the Second World War, representatives from 26 countries gathered. They promised their countries' support in fighting together against the Axis Powers. The Axis Powers were those countries that were on the same side as Germany during the war. This promise was called the "Declaration by United Nations."

U.S. President Franklin D. Roosevelt coined the name "United Nations."

Representatives from 50 countries joined in 1945 in San Francisco. They met at the UN Conference on International Organization. Their job was to create the UN Charter. The charter was signed on June 26, 1945, by representatives from many countries. Some of those countries were China, France, the Soviet Union, the United Kingdom, and the United States. The UN became official on October 24, 1945.

The UN is an organization now made up of people from about 200 countries. Almost every nation in the world is a UN member. Members work to preserve peace by getting along with each other. They also help each other ensure the safety of all people.

The UN Charter, or agreement, is accepted by all member nations. This charter explains the four purposes of the UN. Its first purpose is to maintain peace and security across nations. Its second purpose is to develop friendships among nations. Helping each other solve problems between nations is the UN's third purpose. Its fourth purpose is to be a center for peacefully blending the actions of nations.

The UN does not make laws. It was created to provide ways to help resolve conflict between nations. Every nation in the UN is able to vote on decisions made by the UN. No matter what size

The United Nations headquarters in New York

the country, each gets one vote. Poor countries get one vote like the richer countries do.

Six main groups make up the UN. One of these groups is the International Court of Justice. This court is based at The Hague in the Netherlands. The other five groups are based in New York at the UN headquarters. These groups include the General Assembly and the Security Council. The Economic and Social Council, the Trusteeship Council, and the Secretariat are also based there.

The General Assembly is made up of people from each member nation. This group meets to discuss the world's most urgent problems. In the beginning of the 21st century, over 180 different topics were discussed. Some of these topics included AIDS, the conflict in Africa, and the protection of our environment. The Assembly cannot force nations to correct or fix problems. Its recommendations represent how most of the nations feel about a particular issue. The UN can also help jump start a country's plan to improve.

The Security Council's main role is to maintain international security and peace. Whenever there is a threat to peace, the council may gather. The UN Charter states that all nation members must follow the Security Council's decisions.

The United Nations General Assembly

Representatives from 15 member nations make up the Security Council. Five nations are permanent members. These are China, France, Russia, the United Kingdom, and the United States. The other 10 are elected by the General Assembly. They serve two-year terms. It takes nine yes votes to make a decision formal. If a question involves internal UN practices, it is handled differently. No decision can be made in these cases if even one permanent member votes no.

The Security Council can take steps to make sure its decisions are carried out. It can call for economic sanctions, where a country is given a financial penalty. The Council can also call for a ban on what the country trades. This is called an "embargo." Only rarely has the Council told a member nation it could use "all necessary means." "All necessary means " could include military action.

The Economic and Social Council has 54 members. These 54 members are elected by the General Assembly for three-year terms. This council plans discussions and actions to improve life for all people. It wants to better people's social standing and their finances. It works to develop cooperation between nations. The council also makes recommendations to government policy makers. This group works to prevent crime worldwide, too. It deals with protecting the environment and bettering the treatment of women. The council also tries to control the flow of illegal drugs.

The Trusteeship Council was created to provide supervision for 11 territories. The council's role was to help prepare these territories to govern themselves. By 1994, all Trust Territories had gained independence or had become self-governing. This council, now made up of five permanent members, meets on an as-needed basis. This council would meet if and when a new territory needed help to become self-governing.

The International Court of Justice is the main judicial part of the UN. This legal group is also called the World Court. The General Assembly and the Security Council elect the court's 15 judges. These judges decide disagreements between countries. Member nations can choose to be part of a hearing. If they do take part, they must follow the Court's decision. This Court could consider how to prevent and punish groups who take part in genocide. Genocide is the killing of certain ethnic groups. The Court could also settle an oil trade dispute between two countries.

The Secretariat is the group that carries out the work of the UN. The General Assembly might decide on a new policy. Then the Secretariat decides what needs to happen to make the policy effective. They would then accomplish this work. The General

Assembly, the Security Council, and the other UN bodies direct this group. The Secretary-General oversees this group. Up to about 15,000 people from about 170 countries work for the Secretariat. About half of these are under the regular budget. The other half are brought in under special funding. These UN employees may work at the New York headquarters. Others may work in UN offices in Geneva, Switzerland, in Vienna, Austria, or in Nairobi, Kenya.

The U.S. pays a large part of the dues collected from UN member nations. In the past, the U.S. held back some of its dues. They sometimes did this to show that they didn't approve of a UN decision. They also did this to show that they disliked how the UN handled a certain situation.

After the September 11, 2001, terrorist attacks, the U.S. relied on the UN as never before. The U.S. looked to the UN for support in its war against terrorism. The U.S. dues were lowered, and the U.S. paid the UN much of what it owed. The relations between the U.S. and the UN then improved.

The Inspection Process

UN weapons inspectors work to make the world safe from weapons of mass destruction. The inspectors and their teams are experts on missiles, chemical, and biological weapons. They have different backgrounds and come from different countries. This team includes customs experts, import-export specialists, and people who can speak several languages. On this team, the UN includes people who can tell the difference between right and wrong actions. Doctors, pilots, language experts, and other support staff back up the inspection teams.

Inspection teams are typically made up of four or five people. Major inspection projects could require 20 to 30 team members. Each team includes weapons experts as well as a report writer. The team's job involves everything from tagging equipment to determining if factories are secretly producing weapons. They also set up video cameras and recorders. This equipment allows inspections to continue after the inspectors leave the country. Written reports of the inspectors' findings are forwarded to the UN. Finally, the UN decides what action should be taken based on that report.

A UN Weapons Inspector's helmet

The 1990s UN Weapons Inspections of Iraq

In 1988, former President George H.W. Bush took office. He tried to strengthen the United States-Iraq relationship. In 1990, Iraq surprised the U.S. by invading Kuwait. The former president felt betrayed and sent U.S. military troops into Kuwait in early 1991. Bush wanted to protect U.S. oil interests and liberate Kuwait. The United States and its allies' removal of Iraq from Kuwait was called the Gulf War.

The first phase of the Gulf War was called Operation Desert Shield. Its goal was to free Kuwait and force Iraqi soldiers out of Kuwait. When the UN failed to get Iraq to leave Kuwait peacefully, Operation Desert Storm was launched. The U.S. military and its allies successfully forced Iraq out of Kuwait. Operation Desert Storm lasted less than two months. It was a victory for the U.S. and its allies. Saddam was left in place, but U.S. officials kept an eye on his actions. They did this through a UN agreement that imposed weapons inspections on Iraq.

UN weapons inspectors in the field

In April 1991, Iraq accepted a UN agreement. Saddam said he would allow UN inspectors to search for weapons. The UN Security Council followed up by establishing the UN Special Commission, or UNSCOM.

The members of UNSCOM were first led by Rolf Ekeus of Sweden. They were then led by Richard Butler of Australia. These members represented various nations. Their purpose was to order inspections of Iraq's weapons of mass destruction. Biological and chemical weapons and missiles were to be found. Then these weapons were to be removed and/or destroyed. UNSCOM was to prevent facilities from making weapons, too. Members were directed to work with the International Atomic Energy Agency, IAEA.

The UN created the IAEA in 1957 to be a tool used by various governments. IAEA was to ensure that all countries were using nuclear power for "peaceful uses" only. Its mission from the start was to prevent the spread of nuclear weapons. UNSCOM investigators would search for chemical and biological weapons. IAEA would search for nuclear weapons. These two groups formed the Iraq UN weapons inspections team.

The inspectors were in and out of Iraq during Bush's and then Bill Clinton's presidencies. What the inspectors found was disturbing. Iraq had managed to secretly build a nuclear weapons

Weapon of mass destruction

program. The country was probably only a year away from being able to cause great harm. These nuclear weapons, once built, could have killed thousands of people. The inspectors disarmed the program.

Saddam's reaction to the inspections varied from cooperation to refusal to cooperate. In the mid 1990s, the Iraqi government frustrated the search teams. Saddam's people would close down inspections as the investigators got close to new material. Finally, UNSCOM removed all inspection teams from Iraq at the end of 1998. UNSCOM said that the Iraqi government failed to cooperate with the inspectors.

In response, Bill Clinton, who was now the president of the United States, ordered a cruise missile attack. This attack was called Operation Desert Fox. Clinton wanted to punish Saddam for his lack of cooperation. He also tried to help rebels remove Saddam from leadership. Clinton's plan was not successful. Though Saddam's weapons program was crippled, he remained in place.

Former U.S. President Bill Clinton

UN Weapons Inspections in the 21st Century

In 2001, George W. Bush became president of the United States. It seemed like Saddam Hussein had outsmarted the U.S. He was still in power, and the UN weapons inspectors were gone. Even worse, the U.S. and other countries believed that Saddam was still building forbidden weapons.

The September 11, 2001, terrorist attacks changed the U.S. policy towards Iraq. The U.S. government decided it was time to better protect Americans and their allies. Terrorists and countries that meant to harm others had to be stopped. No longer would groups or governments thought to have forbidden weapons be left alone. The U.S. knew it was important to disarm Iraq. They wanted to disarm all other governments and groups that threatened harm, too.

Before President Bush decided how to disarm Iraq, he looked to the UN for support. The UN had replaced UNSCOM with the UN Monitoring Verification and Inspection Commission, UNMOVIC, in late 1999.

The people who worked for UNMOVIC were all employees of the UN. This was different than those who were part of UNSCOM. UNMOVIC members must be quick workers and know a lot about weapons. They must also show that they can be trusted. Members came from countries around the world. Since 2000, they have been led by Hans Blix of Sweden.

Bush made an important speech to the UN General Assembly on September 12, 2002. He spoke about the common goals of the U.S. and the UN. His goal was to get the nations to help the U.S. force Saddam to disarm. He wanted to use tougher threats against Iraq than the UN had ever used before.

President Bush spoke about the danger that Saddam's government and terrorists posed for the U.S. and other countries. He said, "Our greatest fear is that terrorists will find a shortcut to their mad ambitions when an outlaw regime supplies them with the technologies to kill on a massive scale." Bush pledged, "My nation will work with the UN Security Council to meet our common challenge. If Iraq's regime defies us again, the world must move deliberately, decisively to hold Iraq to account."

Hans Blix led the Iraqi Weapons Inspectors beginning in 2000.

Following Bush's speech, the UN voted to make Iraq disarm. The 2002 UN inspectors were given more power than those who inspected Iraq earlier. These inspectors did not need to give Iraqi officials advanced warning of the inspection locations. They could also take people and families out of Iraq to protect them. The Iraqi people could give information to the inspectors and not worry about their safety. The Iraqis were also required to fully cooperate with the 2002 inspectors.

There were 220 experts from 44 countries qualified to serve on the 2002 inspection team. About 80 of them would be in Baghdad, Iraq's capital, at any one time. Doctors, pilots, language experts, and other staff would support these 80 inspectors. This made the total team count between 120 and 130 in Baghdad.

Investigation teams of four to five or larger would leave the Baghdad office. The locations of the inspection sites were kept secret until the last minute. The element of surprise was necessary. It helped reduce the chance that the Iraqis could hide weapons just before the inspectors' arrival. The inspectors believed that more surprise visits meant truer report results.

Once the investigators reached their assigned sites, their job was to tag equipment. They also had to determine if certain factories were producing chemical weapons parts. Video cameras and recorders were also set up. This allowed the UN to watch the visited sites after the inspectors left.

U.S. government officials were concerned that there were not enough inspectors in Iraq. They were also worried that the types of searches being done were not varied enough.

Some people believed that the U.S. government was determined to start a war with Iraq. This is just what the UN hoped to avoid. President Bush seemed to soften slightly from his pledge to bring about an Iraqi "regime change." A regime change means a change in leadership. At one point, he hinted that the U.S. might leave Saddam in place. This could happen if there was a "change in the regime." This would mean that Saddam had to be truthful and stop building his weapons program.

President Bush said that the U.S. wanted peace but must be prepared for the chance of war. He said, "America will confront gathering dangers early before our options become limited and desperate. By showing resolve today, we are building a future of peace."

U.S. President George W. Bush

Iraqi officials completed a 12,000 page report required by the UN. They forwarded the report to UN representatives in December 2002. The report was to include a list of all Iraqi weapons of mass destruction. This report was important. It would help decide whether the United States and Iraq could settle their differences in a peaceful manner.

Unfortunately, the report did not settle anything. It did not convince President Bush that Iraq had properly disarmed. He wanted the UN to stand behind a U.S.-led attack against the Iraqi government. Some UN countries supported Bush. Others wanted to allow Iraq more time to disarm. Bush realized he no longer had the UN support he had hoped for. He decided to move forward without that backing.

On March 17, 2003, Bush went on T.V. to tell Saddam that he had 48 hours to leave Iraq. If Saddam didn't leave, he would face war. On March 19, the U.S. and its allies began the war against Saddam's regime.

Other UN Weapons Inspections

Stopping the threat of weapons of mass destruction is a difficult and complicated job. It requires cooperation by countries around the world. More than 50 years have passed since the U.S. bombed Japan. To prevent similar disasters, agreements have been reached between nations. Physical security measures and other control systems have been put into place across the globe. For decades, the IAEA has made sure that these agreements are being met by all.

Most countries in the world use nuclear techniques for multiple peaceful purposes. One approved use is electric power generation. Others include food production and medicine. These uses are protected under contracts with the IAEA. Over 40 countries have nuclear reactors. Many facilities also hold nuclear materials that are accounted for.

According to a spokesperson for the IAEA, "Inspectors carry out hundreds of routine accounting and verification activities every year related to nuclear materials and facilities in member states [member nations]." No other inspections in history, though, were watched as closely or by as many people as the 2002 Iraqi inspections were.

Flag of the United Nations

Nuclear power used for a peaceful purpose, providing electricity to people

WEB SITES
WWW.ABDOPUB.COM

Would you like to learn more about UN Weapons Inspectors? Please visit www.abdopub.com to find up-to-date Web site links about UN Weapons Inspectors and the World in Conflict. These links are routinely monitored and updated to provide the most current information available.

International Court of Justice based at The Hague in the Netherlands

Timeline

1945	The United Nations becomes official.
1957	International Atomic Energy Agency (IAEA) is created.
1989–1993	George H.W. Bush is U.S. president.
1990	Iraq invades Kuwait.
1991	The Gulf War begins and ends.
	Kuwait is liberated. Iraq accepts the UN resolution requiring it to end its weapons of mass destruction program. Iraq also agrees to ongoing monitoring. UN Special Commission, UNSCOM, is established.
1993–2001	Bill Clinton is U.S. president.

1998	UN Weapons Inspectors leave Iraq. President Clinton orders "Operation Desert Fox."
1999	Richard Butler completes his term as UNSCOM's Executive Chairman. UN replaces UNSCOM with UNMOVIC, the UN Monitoring and Inspection Commission.
2000	Hans Blix becomes the Executive Chairman of UNMOVIC.
2000	George W. Bush is elected U.S. president.
2001	Terrorists attack the U.S. on September 11.
2002	President Bush secures UN support for holding Iraq more accountable for its weapons of mass destruction program. UN weapons inspectors search Iraq.
2003	President Bush and U.S. allies launch an attack on Iraq on March 19.

Fast Facts

- When the UN was first established in 1945, 51 countries were members. By the early twenty-first century, 191 nations, which represented almost every nation in the world, belonged to the UN.

- The UN was not designed to make laws. Its purpose is to promote peace across the world.

- Former U.S. President Franklin D. Roosevelt first coined the name "United Nations."

- The UN created the International Atomic Energy Agency (IAEA) in 1957 to ensure that countries across the world were using nuclear power only for peaceful purposes.

- In his first year as president, George H.W. Bush signed a secret order that called for a closer relationship between the U.S. and Iraq.

- In 1991, after a 39-day military bombing campaign kicked off the Gulf War, U.S.-led ground troops took only four days to beat the Iraqi army.

- In 1993, the United States Central Intelligence Agency, or CIA, uncovered evidence that showed Iraq was involved in a plan to assassinate President George H.W. Bush.

- The UN weapons inspectors who searched Iraq in 2002, worked from a list that contained hundreds of suspect sites.

- As of 2002, Saddam Hussein had stayed in power through the U.S. presidential terms of Jimmy Carter, Ronald Reagan, George H.W. Bush, Bill Clinton, and George W. Bush.

GLOSSARY

AIDS (Acquired Immune Deficiency Syndrome):
A disease that weakens the immune system. It is caused by the Human Immunodeficiency Virus (HIV).

all necessary means:
Whatever action is necessary; this may include military action.

Axis powers:
Those countries that supported Germany in World War II.

biological weapon:
Bacteria, viruses, fungi, and protozoa used deliberately to infect large portions of the enemy's population.

charter:
A written document outlining the rights and obligations of an organization's members.

chemical weapon:
Highly dangerous man-made substances that are dispersed in liquid or gas forms to harm large portions of the enemy's population.

disarm:
To take away and/or destroy weapons.

Gulf War:
The United States-led military action against Iraq in 1991.

Hiroshima:
A city in Japan that was destroyed in World War II (1945) by the first atomic bomb used in war.

International Atomic Energy Agency (IAEA):
Agency started in 1957 within the United Nations to create and apply international safeguards consistent with promoting the peaceful uses of atomic energy and preventing new nations from making nuclear weapons.

invasion:
The entry of an armed force into enemy territory.

Iraq:
A country in the Middle East led by Saddam Hussein.

League of Nations:
An international organization started in 1920 to promote cooperation and peace across the world. It ended in 1946, when it failed to prevent World War II.

missile:
A weapon that is thrown, fired, or dropped on a target.

nuclear weapon:
An instrument of attack that relies on the energy of atomic nuclei.

Operation Desert Fox:
The cruise missile attack that former President Bill Clinton ordered on Iraq in December 1998; the attack was to punish Saddam for not cooperating with UN weapons inspectors.

policy:
A course of action.
regime:
A government.
security:
Freedom from risk or danger.
terrorism:
The illegal use of violence by a person or a group of people with the intention of intimidating a society or government.
United Nations (UN):
An international organization started in 1945 to promote peace, security, and economic development across the world.
United Nations Monitoring and Verification and Inspection Commission (UNMOVIC):
An organization of UN employees first brought together in 1999 to rid Iraq of its weapons of mass destruction. UNMOVIC replaced UNSCOM.
United Nations Special Commission (UNSCOM):
An organization established in 1991 by the UN to inspect and disarm Iraq of its weapons of mass destruction.
weapon of mass destruction:
An instrument of attack that causes injury and/or death to large numbers of people at one time.

The flags of member nations in front of the UN Headquarters in New York

INDEX

B

Bush, George H.W. 23, 25, 40, 42

Bush, George W. 5, 7, 29, 30, 32-35, 40, 41

Butler, Richard 25, 41

C

Clinton, Bill 25, 27, 28, 40, 41, 43

E

Ekeus, Rolf 25

G

Gulf War 23, 40, 43

H

Hussein, Saddam 7, 10, 11, 23, 25, 27, 29, 30, 33, 35, 43

I

International Atomic Energy Agency (IAEA) 25, 36, 37, 40, 42

Iraq 7, 9, 23, 25, 27, 29, 30, 32, 33, 35, 40-43

L

League of Nations 12

O

Operation Desert Fox 27

R

Roosevelt, Franklin D. 12, 13, 42

U

United Nations (UN) 5, 7, 9, 11-25, 29, 30-33, 35, 37, 39, 40-43

United Nations Charter 14, 16

United Nations Economic and Social Council 16, 18

United Nations General Assembly 16-20, 30

United Nations International Court of Justice 16, 19, 39

United Nations Monitoring Verification and Inspection Commission (UNMOVIC) 30, 41

United Nations Secretariat 16, 19, 20

United Nations Security Council 16, 18, 19, 20, 25, 30

United Nations Special Commission (UNSCOM) 25, 27, 30, 40, 41

United Nations Trusteeship Council 16, 19

W

World War II 12